Of Course They Do!

Boys and Girls Can Do Anything

Marie-Sabine Roger
and Anne Sol

Charlesbridge

Boys don't dance.

What?
Of course
they do!

Boys don't cook.

Are you sure?

Boys don't take care of babies.

Boys don't jump rope.

What's this, then?

Boys don't cry.

Don't they?

Girls don't play sports.

What?
Of course they do!

Girls don't care about cars.

Actually . . .

Girls don't build things.

Just look!

Girls don't know about flying.

Not true!

Boys and girls don't . . . Wait! Of course they do!

To my children, girls and boys.
—M-S. R.

Thanks to the children in the photographs for their patience and enthusiasm: Anouskà Antanasijévic-Kavanagh, Jeanne Barroux, Maxime Brayer, Marius & Simon Giraud, Corto Valfrédini, Laétitia & Alice Véry, and Noé Weiss. Thanks also to their parents and to Anne Barathelemy for their precious collaboration.
—A. S.

2014 First U.S. edition
Text copyright © 2009 by Marie-Sabine Roger and Anne Sol
Photographs copyright © • cover, p. 1, p. 2, p. 6, p. 10, p. 14, p. 18, p. 22, p. 26, p. 30, p. 34 © Anne Sol • pp. 4–5 © Christian Lantry/Getty Images • pp. 8–9 © Vegar Abelsnes Photography/Getty images • pp. 12–13 © Nick North/Comet/Corbis • pp. 16–17 © Al Bello/Getty Images Sport • pp. 20–21 © Seitz Art/Gamma • pp. 24–25 © Ed. Lemaistre/PanoramiC • pp. 28–29 © Gabriel Bouys/AFP • pp. 32–33 © Bruno Barbey/Magnum Photos • pp. 36–37 © 5568/CNES/Gamma • pp. 38–39 © Pixland/Corbis

Published by Charlesbridge
85 Main Street Watertown, MA 02472
(617) 926-0329 • www.charlesbridge.com

First published in France in 2009 by Éditions Sarbacane, 35, rue d'Hauteville, 75010 Paris, France
as *A quoi tu joues?* Copyright © 2009 Éditions Sarbacane. www.editions-sarbacane.com

Library of Congress Cataloging-in-Publication Data
Roger, Marie-Sabine, 1957–
    [A quoi tu joues? English]
    Of course they do!: boys and girls can do anything / Marie-Sabine Roger & Anne Sol; [translated by Nathalie Jelidi].
        p. cm.
    Originally published as: A quoi tu joues? Paris: Editions Sarbacane, 2009.
    Summary: Boys do not cook, and girls cannot play sports—but in this book the pictures tell a different story.
    ISBN 978-1-58089-669-6 (reinforced for library use)
    ISBN 978-1-60734-677-7 (ebook)
1. Girls—Juvenile fiction. 2. Boys—Juvenile fiction. 3. Sex role—Juvenile fiction. 4. Sex differences—Juvenile fiction.
[1. Girls—Fiction. 2. Boys—Fiction. 3. Sex role—Fiction. 4. Sex differences—Fiction.] I. Sol, Anne. II. Jelidi, Nathalie.
III. Title.
PZ7.R62554Of 2014
[E]—dc23   2013004293

Printed in China
(hc) 10 9 8 7 6 5 4 3 2 1

Display type set in Family Dog by PizzaDude.dk
Text type set in Janson by Linotype
Color separations by KHL Chroma Graphics, Singapore
Printed and bound September 2013 by Jade Productions in Heyuan, Guangdong, China
Production supervision by Brian G. Walker
Designed by Whitney Leader-Picone